Where does it come from?

LEGO® brick

Illustrated by
Diane Tippell

Macdonald

3702209689

D0241851

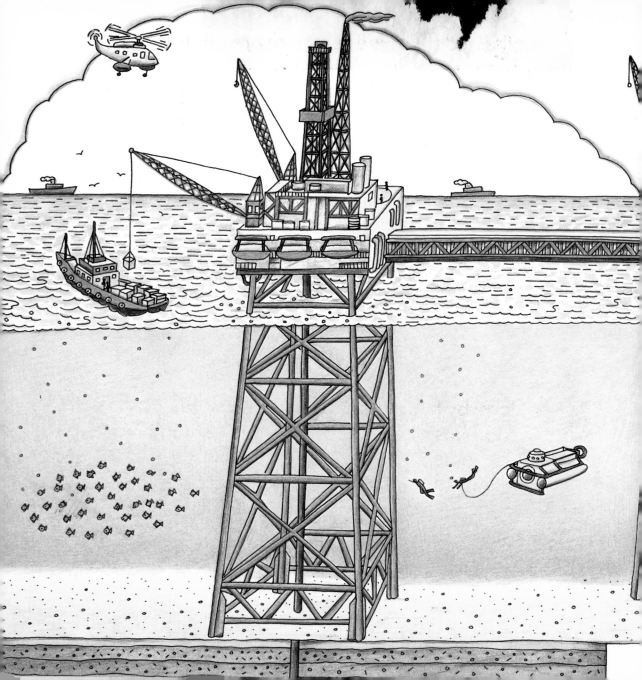

Right out in the middle of the sea there are oil drilling platforms. They push pipes deep down into the rocks under the sea bed to pump up the oil that lies in underground lakes there. Other oil rigs drill on land and in the desert. Here in the ocean, divers go down to check the rig is safe.

The people who work on these rigs live out here for weeks at a time and take it in turns to fly back to land by helicopter for a few days' break. All their food has to come by ship and their rubbish leaves the same way. The big platform is the drilling rig. The smaller one is pumping the oil along the big pipeline on the sea bed back to shore.

The pipeline brings the oil to the refinery. More comes in from other parts of the world in big oil tanker ships. There are hundreds of pipes and tanks, towers and chimneys here and there is some smoke and steam and a strange smell, but you can't see the oil.

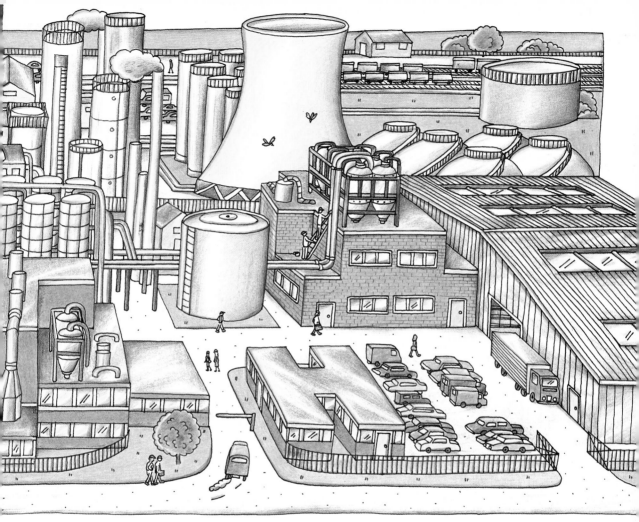

It's inside being heated, cleaned and separated into different parts to be used for things like petrol and plastic. The part of the oil that is turned into plastic has to go through more heating and treating before it can be used. This is done in the chemical plant – the red buildings around the car park.

Inside the chemical plant what started out as oil has now become a fine white powder, though you still can't see it. This is the last stage in making plastic. Upstairs, colour is added to the powder and whirled around in a tank like a giant food mixer until it all melts into a sticky lump. This drops down on to giant rollers which squeeze it out flat. Then it is cooled in a tank of water. Finally another machine chops the coloured plastic up into tiny pellets. These are drawn up a pipe and down through the funnel into big cardboard boxes ready to be taken off to the LEGO factory.

When the boxes of coloured plastic pellets arrive at the LEGO factory the forklift truck driver unloads them from the lorry and piles them up in the store. The store man brings them out on a trolley when they're needed.

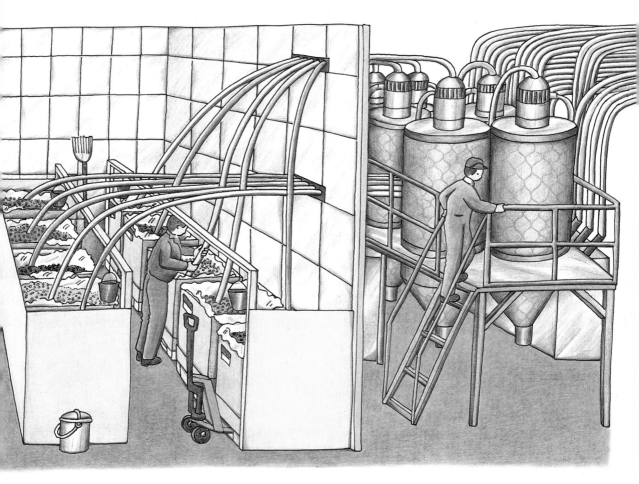

He puts the box in place, opens it and puts the end of a pipe inside. This sucks hard like a vacuum cleaner and draws the tiny plastic pellets up along the pipe and into the big tanks on the other side of the wall. Each tank stores different colour pellets and feeds them out through more pipes to the machines that make the LEGO bricks.

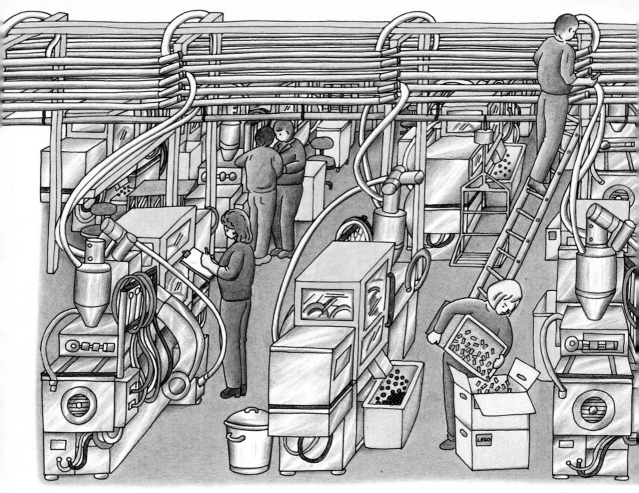

Here are the machines. Each has a mould inside in the shape
of a particular brick. Can you see the pipes bringing the
plastic pellets? Inside the machine the plastic is heated up
until it's soft and then squeezed through a nozzle into the
mould. In no time it cools and goes hard, the mould opens and
there's the finished brick.

It drops into a bin, leaving the mould ready to be filled again. The machine operators are always checking to see that the bricks are coming out right. When a bin is full of bricks they empty it into a box and load the box into one of the yellow hanging cradles which move slowly along the overhead rail to the next part of the factory.

Some LEGO bits are painted or printed by machines — heads get faces on them, bodies get buttons, some bricks have stripes. Machines like this put certain pieces together. It's very clever. The round feeder drums shake the parts into a line and feed them in. They even make sure the bodies are facing the right way.

Each body gets arms, then hands, then a head and 'pop', out at the end falls the half person. Another machine puts the legs on their hinges — you have to put the bodies and legs together. But no matter how clever the machine, it's the operators who are in charge. They have to watch carefully — is everything all right?

Now all the different bricks have to be sorted out. Machines do some of it. The machines in the top row drop one or more pieces at a time into the green boxes passing on the moving belt. At the end of the line the boxes go up the slope and tip up, emptying their bits into plastic bags which come out at the bottom. But the bags have to be made up into the finished LEGO sets...

and it takes people to sort these out. The workers in the packing line put the instructions, different bags and loose bits into the special boxes. Slowly, jumbled heaps of bricks turn into castle sets or car, train or fire-station sets.

The finished sets are ready, the machine seals them up and the workers pack them into big cardboard boxes. These big boxes are marked to show which country they're going to. The leaflets inside have to be in the right language. The forklift truck drivers take the boxes off to the warehouse to be stored.

When they are needed by the toyshops the boxes are loaded
into the back of a container lorry and driven away. Some go
to toyshops in other countries. They may have to travel by
boat or train as well as by lorry to get there.

The LEGO lorry has arrived and just in time. This toyshop is very busy and had sold out of some of the sets. Now Lizzie and Dan's mum will have plenty of sets to choose their birthday presents from. That huge model in the window was built by special designers at the LEGO factory and sent over ready-made. Just imagine having a job building with LEGO bricks!

The birthday tea is over — and the children are having a
LEGO feast. There are big bricks for the baby. Mum and the
twins are doing some complicated building, even grandpa is
having a go. Isn't it strange to think that all these models are
made from oil that was once buried deep under the ground.